Who's Afraid of ™

Grammar?

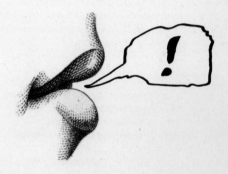

Correct use is not founded on Grammar,
but Grammar on correct use.

Richard Whately, *The Elements of Rhetoric*, 1828

Editor: Stephen Haynes
Editorial assistant: Mark Williams

Published in Great Britain in MMXIII by
Book House, an imprint of
The Salariya Book Company Ltd
25 Marlborough Place, Brighton BN1 1UB
www.salariya.com
www.book-house.co.uk

HB ISBN-13: 978-1-908973-47-4

visit
www.salariya.com
for our online catalogue and
free interactive web books.

Who's Afraid of ™

Grammar?

Not I.

Jacqueline Morley

SALARIYA
BH
BOOK HOUSE

Let us consider how many ideas we owe to the use of speech, how much grammar exercises and facilitates the operations of the mind.

Jean-Jacques Rousseau,
Discourse on Inequality, 1754

Grammar, perfectly understood, enables us, not only to express our meaning fully and clearly, but so to express it as to enable us to defy the ingenuity of man to give our words any other meaning than that which we ourselves intend them to express.

William Cobbett,
A Grammar of the English Language, 1818

I will not go down to posterity talking bad grammar.

Benjamin Disraeli, correcting proofs of his last parliamentary speech, 1881

Forget grammar and think about potatoes.

Gertrude Stein, *How to Write*, 1931

Contents

Preface

IN A TEXT to a friend you can write however you like, but there are some situations – such as applying for a job, or writing an essay or report – where you need to make a good impression on others. This book, and others in the series, will help you to write in a way that teachers, employers and people in authority will approve of.

Grammar rules vary slightly from one English-speaking country to another. What we describe here mainly applies to British English, but we do point out some of the most important differences between British and North American usage. Australian and New Zealand English mostly follow British rules.

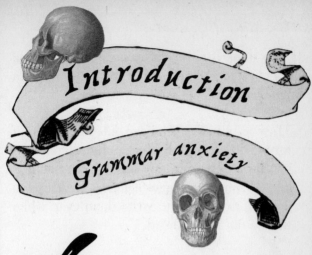

Introduction
Grammar anxiety

ACCORDING to one expert, English grammar has about 3,500 rules. But don't panic: you've probably picked up most of these rules already, without even realising. You may not remember what the definition of a subject or an object is, but the chances are you always get your subjects and objects the right way round.

Most of us know how to make ourselves understood when we're speaking face to face, but when it comes to writing we still worry that our grammar will let us down. And that's where this little book comes in. It doesn't attempt to cover all those 3,500 rules, but concentrates on the ones English speakers find confusing.

If you think English grammar is complicated, just compare it to some other European languages:

• Most verbs in English have only four different forms: *like, likes, liked, liking*; in most languages you have to learn many sets of verb endings, and in some languages (such as French) you have to remember to write them even when they're not pronounced.

• No English noun has more than four forms: *son, sons, son's, sons'*. In German you have to learn four different cases, each with a singular and a plural form; in Russian there are at least six cases (some experts recognise nine); in Hungarian there are 18! (Cases are the different forms a noun or pronoun takes according to the role it is playing in a sentence.)

• English is almost the only European language where you don't have to worry whether a noun is masculine, feminine or neuter, or whether an adjective is masculine, feminine, neuter, singular or plural.

Does that make you feel any better?

Pedant alert!

Pet peeve

Look out for our **PET PEEVE** symbol. There is a certain kind of person (language experts call them *peevologists*) who loves nothing better than to pick holes in other people's use of language. 'Pet peeves' are particular mistakes (or so-called mistakes) which cause these people to get dangerously steamed up and, in extreme cases, write letters to the *Daily Telegraph*.

This book is not meant to turn you into a peevologist yourself – perish the thought – but it could help you to avoid needlessly provoking such people.

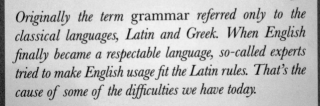

Grammar trivia

Originally the term grammar *referred only to the classical languages, Latin and Greek. When English finally became a respectable language, so-called experts tried to make English usage fit the Latin rules. That's the cause of some of the difficulties we have today.*

Sentences

'This is not a proper sentence'. We've all had remarks like that scrawled across our homework at some time or other. The English teacher wasn't being a peeve but was simply enforcing a rule that shouldn't be broken.

OK, but how do we know what is a sentence and what isn't? The rule used to be:

A sentence is a string of words expressing a complete thought.

Although that's true, it's too vague. How do we judge when a thought is complete enough? For instance, if you ask someone to do you a favour and they reply 'Not on your nelly', that's a pretty complete expression of how they feel, but it isn't a sentence.

These are the grammarians' rules:

1. A sentence must have a subject and a predicate.

2. The predicate must contain a finite verb whose action is performed by or experienced by the subject.

Jargon buster

subject *The person, thing or idea that the sentence is talking about.*
predicate *The part of the sentence that has something to say about the subject.*
verb *The part of the predicate that expresses what the subject is doing or what is being done to it.*

*A **finite verb** has a subject and a tense.* I go, he goes *(present tense),* they went *(past tense) are finite.* To go, going, gone *have no tense and are not finite.*

*Some verbs may have an **object**, which denotes the person, place or thing affected by the verb, although a sentence can be complete without an object in its predicate.*

Great writers can afford to ignore the rules now and then, as Charles Dickens did when he opened his novel *Bleak House* like this:

> London. Michaelmas term lately over, and the Lord Chancellor sitting in Lincoln's Inn Hall. Implacable November weather. . . . Fog everywhere. Fog up the river. . . . Fog on the Essex Marshes, fog on the Kentish heights.

He keeps this up for three paragraphs: sentence after sentence and not a finite verb in sight, although you could argue that a ghostly *is* or *was* is understood in all of them. Dickens was creating a special effect; he didn't make a habit of writing like this, and neither should we.

Which all goes to show what a slippery customer a sentence is to pin down.

Pet peeve

(Now that's a sentence peeves won't approve of, because it has *which* as its subject. *Which* isn't a noun, they'll say (see 'Nouns', pages 21–28), and shouldn't be encouraged to behave like one. Well, I've written it now so I'll let it stand.)

Sentences plain and fancy

• **Simple sentences** contain one clause:

Our engagement was announced.

• **Compound sentences** contain two clauses which could have stood alone as complete sentences but are linked by a joining word such as *and* or *but*:

Our engagement was announced last night and my parents sighed with relief.

• **Complex sentences** contain a main clause which makes the basic statement, and one or more other clauses that expand it. These would make no sense if they stood alone, so they are called *subordinate* clauses:

Our engagement, which came as a huge relief to my parents, was announced when we were all at home for Christmas.

What's a clause?

A clause is a sentence or any part of a sentence that contains a subject and a finite verb that agrees with it.

13

Well-behaved words

Besides having a meaning, each word in a sentence has what grammarians call its *function*, by which they mean the job it is doing in that particular sentence. There are eight categories of jobs, known as the eight *parts of speech*, and you can tell which category a word belongs to by seeing how it behaves in a sentence.

• **Nouns** are words that name things. 'Things', in this sense, includes:

• people (mother, magician, murderer, Florence Nightingale, Frank Sinatra)

• places (marshland, Denmark, Trafalgar Square)

• creatures and objects (giraffe, screwdriver, umbrella)

• and things that exist only in the mind (impatience, justice, memory, mathematics). The latter are called *abstract nouns*.

When we refer to one thing, a tree for instance, we are using the noun *tree* in its singular form. If we want to refer to more than one of them we use its plural form, *trees*.

• **Pronouns**, such as *you*, *me*, *them*, *hers*, etc., are used in place of nouns to avoid tiresome repetition. Without them, we'd have to say:

> I had breakfast with the Queen and the Queen said the Queen liked the Queen's milk poured into the Queen's cup before the tea.

• **Verbs** tell what's going on in a sentence. They are often described as 'doing words', which is rather misleading as some verbs express a state of mind or of being rather than an action. Active words like *kill*, *explore*, *dissect* are easily recognised as verbs:

> Worker bees *kill* drones.
> Scott *explored* Antarctica.
> The science class *dissected* a frog.

But words like *is*, *seems*, *thinks* are also verbs:

> I *think* you are wrong.
> He *seems* a reasonable person.
> The rain *is* depressing.

15

• **Adjectives** give more information about nouns:

> an *amazing* magician, a *useless* screwdriver, a *crowded* Trafalgar Square

• **Adverbs** tell us more about verbs, such as how, when or where their action takes place:

> He ate *greedily*.
> He ate *too much yesterday*.
> He drops crumbs *everywhere*.

They can also provide more information about adjectives or about other adverbs:

> He is a *remarkably* careless eater.
> He ate that *astonishingly* quickly.

• **Prepositions** are words like *at*, *in*, *by*, *down*, *under*, which we put before a noun or pronoun to show its relationship to some other person, thing or action in the sentence:

> I hid it *under* the bed.
> He had collapsed *by* the lamp post.

• **Conjunctions**, such as *and*, *or*, *but*, *because*, *although*, are linking words. They join two or more words, phrases or clauses:

16

Help me top *and* tail the beans.

He didn't leave it at home *but* at the pool.

None of them stopped me lighting the fire with petrol, *although* they all said later how stupid I'd been.

• **Interjections** are words thrown in to express an emotion or reaction:

Hello!
Phew, it's hot in here.
Wow, I love your dress.

They can consist of more than one word:

My goodness!
Oh–my–God! (if you're American)

Versatile words

Many words have more than one way of behaving. Some can appear in one sentence as a verb and in another as a noun; some double as adjectives and adverbs. To know how a word is behaving in a particular sentence, you have to look at the work it is doing. Ask yourself which of the parts of speech described above it matches:

17

I *fancy* sausages for supper. (verb)
I'm not putting up with her *fancy* attitudes.
(adjective)

The *bulge* in his pocket gave the game away.
(noun)
If you squeeze it in the middle it will *bulge* at
both ends. (verb)

The next train is the *fast* one. (adjective)
If you don't run *fast* we'll miss it. (adverb)

He went *outside* to smoke. (adverb)
He dropped his cigarette butt *outside* the gate.
(preposition)

It's easy to use words in this way in English,
because most English words don't have a shape
that clearly says 'this is a verb' or 'this is a noun'.
Using nouns as verbs is second nature to English
speakers. You can:

Google on the Internet
partner someone
text them a message
source your vegetables from organic suppliers

Nouns used as adjectives – *the world situation, the
Australia tour* – are a headline-writer's joy:

ENGLAND SIDE CAPTAIN
SELECTION DIFFICULTY

and are popular in 'government speak' (it's catching!):

Surplus government chemical-warfare vapour detection kits.

You can use an adjective as a noun:

He threw a *wobbly*.
Don't be a *silly*.

or as an adverb:

You're *plain* stupid.
That's *dead* easy.
He's *barking* mad.

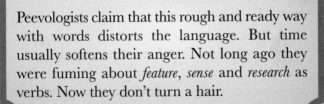

Does it matter?

Peevologists claim that this rough and ready way with words distorts the language. But time usually softens their anger. Not long ago they were fuming about *feature*, *sense* and *research* as verbs. Now they don't turn a hair.

Keep them in order

In many languages the form of a noun when it acts as a subject, for example, differs from its form when it's an object. These changes are called *inflections*. In a highly inflected language you can put words pretty much where you like in a sentence and their meaning will be the same. English has few inflections, so you can't do this: *Banquo murdered Macbeth* is not the same as *Macbeth murdered Banquo*. In English it is the word order that tells you who is murdering whom, so it's important to put words in the order that matches what you want to say.

This is easy in simple sentences, but watch out when there are extra phrases about. Keep them next to the word they relate to, or you could end up with something like the old joke about a man with a wooden leg called Jones. Here's an excerpt from an official report, quoted by Sir Ernest Gowers in his sometimes very funny book *The Complete Plain Words*:

> I have discussed the question of stocking the proposed poultry plant with my colleagues.

Simpler to say 'I have talked with my colleagues about stocking the proposed poultry plant.'

Nouns can be used:

- **as the subject of a sentence:**
  This *book* isn't teaching me anything.

- **as the object of a verb:**
  It couldn't teach a *grandmother* to suck eggs.

- **as the indirect object of a verb:**
  She gave *eggs* the thumbs down for breakfast.
  (meaning 'She gave the thumbs down to eggs.')

- **in apposition (where two nouns are equated with each other):**
  Eggs, an important *element* in any diet, are nourishing for the elderly.

- **in speaking directly to someone:**
  Grandmother, eat up your omelette.

Unruly plurals

Most English nouns form the plural by adding an *-s* (*coat/coats*), or an *-es* if this makes them

21

easier to say (*match/matches*). But some nouns show they're plural by changing their form:

mouse/mice, man/ men, foot/feet, goose/geese

These are leftovers from the time when English was a highly inflected language (see page 20).

Some plurals don't change at all:

sheep/sheep, swine/swine, deer/deer, cod/cod

Some nouns have two plurals with differing meanings:

Fish [as a class] aren't found in the Dead Sea.

The fishes [as individuals] answered, with a grin, | 'Why, what a temper you are in!'
(Lewis Carroll)

People looks singular but is actually plural – you have to say *people are*. Yet this plural noun has a plural of its own, as in *the peoples of the world*.

Certain nouns, such as *trousers, scissors, binoculars, pants, spectacles*, do not have a singular form except when they are used as adjectives:

trouser suit, scissor movement, spectacle lenses

(Though you may hear *a trouser* or *a pant* in fashion-industry jargon.)

It's most important to know whether you're making a statement about one thing or several, because a basic rule of grammar is that the subject and the verb must match, or 'agree':

A monkey has snatched my banana.
(singular subject, singular verb)

Monkeys have no concept of personal property.
(plural subject, plural verb)

Some nouns – like *Parliament, government, department, committee, firm, team* – can be thought of as either singular (one organisation) or plural (a collection of separate people). These are called 'collective nouns'. So, should you say *the Government has decided* or *the Government have decided*? The usual solution is to use a singular verb when you're thinking of the institution as a whole:

Parliament *has* been dissolved.

and a plural verb when the emphasis is on the actions of its individual members:

Parliament *have* been debating the matter.

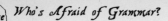

But this plural use is rare in American English, and British peevologists also object to it.

What you must not do is change course halfway:

> The firm *has* given an undertaking that in the event of *their* needing to cut production there will be no redundancies.

The writer has chosen the singular *has*, so should have used *its* rather than *their* – though this author certainly scores peeve points for a correctly used gerund (see page 56).

There are some nouns plural in form – *the United States*, for example – that take a singular verb because they are thought of as an entity:

> The United States *is* putting forward a proposal.

A sitting target

Sometimes a pronoun decides the matter. Sir Ernest Gowers pointed out that it would sound odd to say The committee leaves its hats in the hall, *and rather startling to say* The committee were smaller when I sat on them.

A double subject linked by 'and' – *heaven and earth, a man and his mother* – normally needs a plural verb. But when the two nouns form a single idea, like *bubble and squeak* or *the long and the short of it*, they are treated as singular:

Is fish and chips all right for supper?

Sometimes the choice of singular or plural affects the meaning: *Bread and butter is on the table* does not tell you quite the same thing as *Bread and butter are on the table*.

Foreign plurals can be tricky. *Criteria* and *phenomena* are words borrowed from Greek. They are Greek plurals and must have a plural verb:

The criteria for acceptance *are* strict.

Their singular forms are *criterion* and *phenomenon:*

A phenomenon of this kind *is* inexplicable.

On the other hand, *agenda*, a Latin plural (whose singular would be *agendum*), has for some reason been granted citizenship in English and become singular. No-one would write *The agenda for the meeting are not yet decided*. It now has a regular English plural, *agendas*.

25

Crisis is a Latin singular noun. In English we keep its Latin plural, *crises*.

Data is a Latin plural. Many people, especially scientists, insist that we should write *The data are inconclusive*. But others, particularly in America, allow it as a singular: *Firm data is not available.* It seems that the jury is out on *data*.

Plurals that express an amount are often treated as singular:

Five pounds is all I can afford.

If you say *Here are five pounds*, you are probably counting them out one by one.

With compound nouns like *court martial, passer-by, mother-in-law,* the general rule is that the plural *s* goes with the main element in the noun phrase: *mothers-in-law, passers-by*. Where there is no obvious main element, the *s* attaches itself to the final word of the group: *get-togethers, hand-me-downs, takeovers.* With some nouns we can choose, measuring ingredients in *spoonsful* or *spoonfuls*.

Why not *court martials*? Peevologists gleefully point out that *martial* is an adjective and English adjectives have no plural form.

What's a compound noun?

A compound noun is a noun composed of two or more elements which are complete words in themselves.

Nouns can get possessive

You may be surprised to learn that in correct English you have to cope with four different forms of a noun. There is a singular form and a plural form:

  cat (singular), cats (plural)

Then there is a possessive form, and that comes in singular and plural varieties too:

  the cat's whiskers (the whiskers of one cat)
  the cats' whiskers (more than one cat)

You can see that the singular possessive is made by adding an apostrophe and an *s*. But to make the plural you don't need both a plural *s* and a possessive *s* – just keep the one *s* and hang the apostrophe on the end of the word.

Some plural nouns (*children, men, mice*) don't have a plural *s*. To make the possessive plural you add both the apostrophe and the *s*:

the children's shoes
the men's appearance

Proper nouns that end in *s* are a problem: do you write *St Thomas' Hospital* or *St Thomas's Hospital*? *Keats's poetry* or *Keats' poetry*? The usual rule nowadays is to add both the apostrophe and the second *s*, though the second *s* may be left out in the case of classical names like Demosthenes. It's also omitted in the set expression *for goodness' sake*.

An apostrophe too far

The worst mistake of all, with the possessive apostrophe, is to put it in a word that is not a possessive but a simple plural:

Lovely tomatoe's. Only £1.20.

Pet peeve

This sort of thing appears so often on vegetable stalls that it has become known as the 'greengrocer's apostrophe'. How the peevologists sneer!

28

Pronouns, you'll recall, are words that can be used in place of a noun. There are various kinds:

• **Personal pronouns**, *I*, *you*, *he*, *she*, *we*, *they*, take the place of nouns naming people:

Shakespeare was born in 1564; *he* died in 1616.

It is also a personal pronoun; it refers to things or animals, and sometimes to babies:

The infant was bawling so I gave *it* a bottle.

Unlike nouns, some personal pronouns change their form according to whether they stand for the subject or the object in a sentence:

I am busy. Don't bother *me*.
He is in a foul mood. Don't go near *him*.
She is amazing. There is no one like *her*.
We are going. Are you coming with *us*?
They are broken. You can't use *them*.

29

But *you* and *it* stay the same, whether they are acting as the subject or the object.

- **Possessive pronouns** show ownership:

  my idea, *your* muddle, *his* disappearance, *her* opportunity, *its* forepaws, *their* underpants

They also have special forms which can stand on their own, without being followed by a noun:

  The idea was *mine*.
  This is *his* but that is *hers*.
  Yours are all over the place.
  Theirs got lost.

And they have a 'reflexive' form that refers back to the subject of the sentence:

  I did it *myself*.
  Don't kid *yourself*.
  We must ask *ourselves* this.

- **Demonstrative pronouns** point things out:

  This is how you do it.
  I'll have *that*.
  These are the best.
  I wouldn't choose *those*.

• **Relative pronouns**, *who, whom, whose, which* or *that*, refer back to a noun just used and introduce a subordinate clause giving more information about the noun.

I chose the plum *which* felt ripest.

• **Interrogative pronouns**, *when, who, whom, whose, which* or *what*, introduce a question:

Whose side are you on?
What are you up to in there?

Never use *what* as a relative pronoun, unless you want to sound like Ernie Wise with his famous catchphrase 'this play what I wrote'.

Trouble with pronouns

A pronoun is like an understudy: without a main player to act for, its existence is meaningless. Make sure you give it a noun to represent:

He only bought one lottery ticket and was amazed to win it.

It can't be standing for the lottery ticket: he'd bought that and didn't need to win it. So *it* is left adrift with nothing to relate to.

But there are certain expressions in which a pronoun is used without referring to any noun:

They say that spring is late this year.
I think *it* will stay fine.

The he/she problem

English does not have a personal pronoun that means both *he* and *she*. In the past this was not considered a problem: statements using *he*, *him* or *his* were understood to refer to women too:

A student who is a high achiever can get his diploma in two years.

Nowadays this is no longer acceptable (except to hardline peevologists). Feminists point out that the sentence just quoted implies that high-achieving students are unlikely to be women.

The *he or she* solution is clumsy:

A student can get his or her results posted to him or her if he or she provides a stamped, addressed envelope.

Today's answer to the problem is often:

A student who is a high achiever can get their diploma in two years.

Pet peeve

It's a neat solution, but peevologists loathe it because a singular noun has been given a plural pronoun. It is becoming acceptable even in writing, but to be on the safe side try to rephrase your sentence to avoid it. No-one can object to:

Students who are high achievers can get their diplomas in two years.

Here's an example of what *not* to write, from a notice seen in a clinic:

Any man can donate sperm, provided they are aged between 18 and 41.

He is the only appropriate pronoun here, and sperm of that age would be past its shelf life.

Pronoun strings

Too many pronouns in a row can make it unclear who is doing what:

As soon as he saw him he started to shout.

Who shouted: he who saw, or he who was seen?

Vague relations

Relative pronouns sometimes wrongly attach themselves to the nearest noun, whether they are really related to it or not:

> She shook the dust out of the curtains, upon which everyone began to blow their noses.

In this unfortunate case, *which* does not relate to anything in the first clause but is part of the adverbial phrase that introduces the second. The best solution is to split the sentence in two:

> She shook the dust out of the curtains. Upon this, everyone began to blow their noses.

Mistaken identities

The pronouns *your*, *our*, *their* and *its* are sometimes confused with similar-sounding words that have quite different meanings:

> Your not the only one.

Wrong! The writer should have used *you're* (the contracted form of *you are*).

> I think their lovely.

Wrong! It should be *they're* (short for *they are*).

Come round to are place.

Wrong! It should be *our*, which is pronounced like *are* in some varieties of English.

Pet peeve

Lots of people have a problem with *its* and *it's*, and it's easy to see why. *Its* is a possessive pronoun; it means 'belonging to it'. So it's reasonable to think it should have an apostrophe, like *the dog's* meaning 'belonging to the dog' – reasonable, but wrong.

There are two simple rules which will help you sort your *its* from your *it's*:

1. Most possessive pronouns don't have an apostrophe. We write *his* not *hi's*, *hers* not *her's*, *theirs* not *their's*. (Unfortunately there are a few exceptions: one's, someone's, nobody's…) So the correct possessive of *it* is *its*:

The elephant raised its trunk.

2. We use an apostrophe to show that something has been missed out of a word:

It's going to rain.

35

It's is the shortened form of *it is*. The apostrophe is indicating that an *i* has dropped out of *is*. (*It's* can also stand for *it has*, as in *It's rained in the night*.)

Pet peeve

The 'my husband and I' problem

The Queen often says that, so surely it must be right? Well, very often it isn't. The trouble may stem from the childhood mistake of saying 'Me and Jim did so and so.' Children were told that that was not only wrong but 'common' – that adults who said that sort of thing were ignorant. So the idea got about that 'me and Jim' phrases should be avoided at all costs: the posh version, in all cases, had to be 'Jim and I'. This idea is now so widespread that even people whose grammar is usually up to scratch can be heard using it wrongly. A teacher might say:

These rules have been drawn up by the headmaster and I.

If you take *the headmaster* out of the sentence you are left with *These rules have been drawn up by I*, which is obviously wrong. The teacher should have said:

These rules have been drawn up by the headmaster and me.

36

We know in our bones that phrases like *to me, by me, for me, between you and me and the gatepost*, are correct, but somehow we lose sight of this when something comes between the preposition and the *me*. Don't be distracted; write:

> There is no rift between my brother and me.
> It will make no difference to Ruth and me.
> With love from mother and me.

However, don't overcompensate. It is correct to say *Ruth and I are at each other's throats*, because in this sentence the pronoun is acting as part of the subject, so we need its subject form: *I*.

Blame the Bard

Even Shakespeare didn't always get it right:

> My bond to the Jew is forfeit; and since in paying it, it is impossible I should live, all debts are clear'd between you and I.

> *The Merchant of Venice*, Act III scene ii

Verbs

The verb is the heart of a sentence; without it, a group of words is just a phrase.

No verb can be without a subject. In commands like *Get out!* or *Stand clear!*, which have no obvious subject, the subject is understood to be 'you'.

Verbs, like nouns, come in categories:

• **Transitive verbs** express actions done to someone or something else. *I squashed* does not mean much until the speaker goes on to say *I squashed the earwig. The earwig* is the object of *squashed*. Transitive verbs need an object in order to make sense.

• **Intransitive verbs** are more independent creatures. They make sense without an object. Indeed, they never have one:

He slouched badly.

Badly is not an object that he slouched; it is an adverb describing how he slouched.

Many verbs can be transitive or intransitive according to how they're used. Compare *I sang divinely* (intransitive; *divinely* is an adverb) with *I sang encores till my throat was sore* (transitive: *encores* is the object).

The verb *to be* is intransitive and so, like all intransitive verbs, it cannot have an object. In the sentence *I am a hopeless case*, 'a hopeless case' is not an object that is being 'ammed'. It is what grammarians call the 'complement' of the verb *to be*, by which they mean that it is filling out the statement begun (in this example) with *I am*.

Indirect objects

This sentence appears to have two objects:

The warden gave the car a penalty ticket.

The ticket – the thing that was given – is the true object, or 'direct object', of the verb. The car is the indirect object: not the thing given, but the recipient of the giving. Pronouns can be indirect objects too, as in *I sent her* (indirect object) *a letter* (direct object).

The infinitive

To be, to totter, to gasp, to disappear – these are verbs in their infinitive form, easily recognised in many contexts by the *to* that comes before it. The infinitive is the basic verb, without alterations to express person, number and tense – the verb in its raw state, you might say.

The verbs *shall, will, can, may* and *must* are exceptions. They have no infinitives.

Infinitives are versatile: although they are verbs, they can also act as nouns, and can behave rather like adjectives or adverbs:

Getting personal

A verb has three 'persons' and each of these has two 'numbers', singular and plural.

First person: singular I, *plural* we.

Second person, singular and plural: you.

Third person: singular he, she *or* it, *plural* they.

To forgive is often hard. (noun)

She is someone to avoid. (like an adjective, describing what kind of person she is)

He only does it to annoy. (like an adverb, telling why he does it)

Auxiliary verbs

Auxiliary *means 'helping'. Auxiliary verbs help other verbs to function.* To be, to have, can, may, shall, will *and* must *act as auxiliaries. You can see how helpful they are by looking at the number of meanings they allow us to get out of just one verb:*

she talks	she does talk
she is talking	she can talk
she may talk	she has talked
she has been talking	she did talk
she had talked	she had been talking
she will talk	she should have talked
she may have talked	she might have talked

And there are still several other possibilities.

Participles, present and past

• The present participle always ends in *-ing*: *sleeping, thinking, bouncing*. It is used with an auxiliary verb to express an action that is continuous – that is, not sudden but going on over a period of time:

> You will be sleeping in my bed.
> I am seeing double.
> They were bouncing on the sofa.

A present participle can also act as an adjective: *an overwhelming performance, a falling leaf.*

• The past participle usually ends in *-ed* – *disappointed, defused, decided* – though there are plenty that do not (see opposite). Like the present participle, it needs the help of an auxiliary in order to function as a verb:

> He has disappointed everyone.
> The police had already defused the bomb.
> The jury will have decided by tomorrow.

It can also serve as an adjective: *a disappointed man, a defused bomb, a decided look.*

Verbs with past participles that do not end in *-ed* are said to be 'irregular' (because they do not obey the rules). Here are just a few examples:

Infinitive	*Past participle*
to fall	fallen
to blow	blown
to choose	chosen
to build	built
to bring	brought
to weep	wept
to lay	laid
to make	made
to do	done
to kneel	kneeled *or* knelt
to hang	hanged *or* hung
to dream	dreamed *or* dreamt

Where there is a choice, the *-ed* form is usually favoured in American English.

A few past participles that are regular in British English have irregular forms in American usage:

to dive	dove
to plead	pled
to fit	fit
to sneak	snuck

This is most irregular!

Some verbs are irregular in other ways as well:

Infinitive	Past tense	Past participle
To go	I went	I have gone

The verb to be *is irregular in all sorts of of ways:*

I am, you are, she is, I was, I have been.

Gerunds

Sometimes you'll find an *-ing* word behaving as a noun:

I hate flying. (object)
Rotating makes me dizzy. (subject)

These verbal nouns are called *gerunds*. Though they look like present participles, they are not the same grammatically. They do quite different work, as you'll find in the 'Troubles with verbs' section below (page 56).

Tenses

If you say *I fall over whenever I get up*, you are using the verb *to fall* in its present tense: you are dizzy now. If you say *I fell over several times yesterday*, you are using the verb in its past tense.

In English, those are the only tenses you can indicate by altering the form of the verb. If you want to predict how you'll be feeling tomorrow, you need a future tense. This can only be made by using the auxiliary verbs *will* and *shall*:

I shall be better before long.
He will take time to get over it.

The verb *to be* is used as an auxiliary to form the continuous present (denoting an action which is in progress now):

I am falling.

As well as the simple past – *I fell* – there is a compound past made with the past participle and the present tense of the auxiliary *to have*:

I have fallen over in the kitchen.

This tense is known as the 'present perfect' because it implies that the past action is still affecting the present – you are still on the floor waiting for help – whereas the simple past, *I fell*, suggests that the action is over – you have got up. (American speakers are much more likely to use the simple past in both cases.)

If you want to refer to something that happened before the recent events you're discussing, you need a tense that goes further back in time. This is the past perfect (or pluperfect) tense, made with the past tense of *to have* and the past participle:

I remembered I had fallen over in the same place the year before.

The future perfect expresses something that will have happened by some future time:

You will have been waiting hours by the time I get to you.

Both the continuous present and the ordinary present can express the future; so can the present tense of *to be*, followed by *going to*:

The bus is leaving very shortly.
The bus leaves in an hour.
She is going to start nursery school next week.

Moods

When you make a straightforward statement you are using the **indicative** mood; when you give an order – *Let me go!*, *Nobody move!* – you are using the **imperative** mood. You are in the right mood each time without knowing it.

The **subjunctive** mood has two uses:

• To express hypothetical situations:

If he were to have the operation it wouldn't do him any good.

This could be termed the 'were' subjunctive because it always uses the verb *were*:

I wish I were prime minister.

If you were prime minister the country would be in a mess.

If he were to vote for you he'd need his head examined.

If we were to elect you we'd soon regret it.

If you were all to lose your seats it wouldn't matter.

47

If they were in the cabinet we'd see some changes.

You can see that, except in the *I* and the *he/she/it* forms, this is the same as the normal past tense.

• To express demands or requests.

To get this right, you need to know that the present subjunctive of *to be* is always *be*, and that for all other verbs it is the same as their normal present tense, except that the *he/she/it* form drops its final -*s*:

My parents insist that I be home by midnight.

We demand that we be heard.

He agreed to my request that my daughter take the exam again.

If you're a speaker of British English, these examples probably strike you as old-fashioned. You'd be more likely to say and write (quite correctly) *We demand to be heard* and *My parents insist I should be home by midnight.* Even the 'were' subjunctive is often jettisoned in conversation – *I wish I was prime minister* – though you should use it in writing.

So, provided you remember the 'were' rule, the subjunctive is nothing to worry about. On the eastern side of the Atlantic it has become a rare species, not often spotted, though in America it is still very much alive and well.

Don't be too passive

Sometimes the subject of a verb is not the person or thing performing the action, but the thing or person affected by the action. The verb is then said to be in the **passive voice**:

I squashed the earwig. (active voice: the subject is the person who did the squashing)

The earwig was squashed by me. (passive voice: the subject is the thing squashed)

Passive verbs are often felt to lack the force and directness of active ones.

Because they sound more measured and detached, passive statements are favoured in scientific and official communications, such as this from a list of parking offences:

The vehicle was left in a parking place without payment of the charge indicated by a parking token duly affixed to a valid permit/parking card displayed on the vehicle.

Translated, that means 'You parked your car without showing proof of payment.' There is not much to be said for this 'officialese' style. Wherever you can, use the active form of a verb instead of the passive.

But there are cases in which the passive is better. You might be happier getting a letter saying 'Two months' rent is owing to us and is due to be paid by June 30th' than one which said 'You owe me two months' rent and must pay me by the end of the month.' In the first sentence, the request for payment is tactfully disguised as a useful piece of information; the second one sounds more like an accusation.

Passive aggression

An inspired use of the passive is achieved by Lorelei Lee, the dumb-blonde heroine of Anita Loos's comic novel Gentlemen Prefer Blondes. *Lorelei is recording her life-story in her diary. Referring to one of her more indiscreet actions, she writes: 'When Mr Jennings became shot . . .' (He wasn't fatally injured, only wounded.)*

Trouble with verbs

• The verb must agree with the subject (as we mentioned under nouns):

My favourite supper is kippers.
(singular subject, singular verb)

Kippers are my favourite supper.
(plural subject, plural verb)

Be consistent. Don't write stuff like this:

Pet peeve

The committee has all the facts before it that relate to the subject and have no reason to delay coming to a decision.
(singular *has* and *it* followed by plural *have*)

• Two singular nouns linked by *and* need a plural verb. But if the nouns have blended into one idea in the writer's mind this rule is easily forgotten:

All this criticism and argument is going to scupper the project.

There are two nouns in the subject – *criticism* and *argument* – so the verb should be *are*.

51

Pet peeve

• Writers are sometimes confused when something plural comes between a singular subject and its verb. The plural 'pulls' the verb into the wrong number:

As far as teaching students of many different nationalities are concerned, there is a problem.

The subject of the first verb is the singular *teaching*, not the plural *students* or *nationalities*, so the verb should be singular.

The opposite mistake is just as common:

The results in history this year is very poor.

The subject is *results*, not *history* or *year*, and the plural subject needs a plural verb.

• *One*, used as the subject of a verb, has such an irresistible pull that in certain cases even the peevologists have given up: *More than one question was asked* is accepted as correct, although logically *more than one* cannot be singular.

But they might frown on *One of the days that is really busy is Wednesday*, on the grounds that *really busy* relates to *days*, not to *one*, so the verb should be *are*. Yet we'd all agree with the peevologists in saying *one of the hats that are being worn this year*, because the subject 'feels' plural.

Pet peeve

• *None* traditionally has a singular verb (though this rule is not widely observed today). If you remember that it originally meant 'not one', you will see why:

> Of the likely suspects, none is going to be charged.

• *Either* and *neither*, which are both singular, can be tricky when followed by *of*, as that provides them with an alluring plural noun:

> Neither of the questions have been answered.
> Either of these options are likely to fail.

But both these sentences need a singular verb: *Neither . . . has, Either . . . is.*

Trouble with complements

The complement of the verb *to be* rarely causes any problems. But peevologists object that it's wrong to say *It's me* or *That's him*, since *me* and *him* are object forms and the verb *to be* can't have an object. We should be using the subject forms, *It's I* and *That's he*.

Few people talk like that these days. (Though there are exceptions. If you make a telephone call and ask to speak to Ms Smith, a British person will usually reply 'Speaking,' but an American will often say 'This is she.') But in writing it's best to observe the traditional rule:

It was I who was to blame.

Stop thief!

The poet Richard Harris Barham (1788–1845) makes this point in his Ingoldsby Legends *about the thieving jackdaw of Rheims:*

His eye so dim, so wasted each limb,
  That, heedless of grammar, they all cried,
    'That's him!'

Shall and *will*: which should you choose?

The rule (which gets broken all the time without much damage being done) states that, after *I* and *we*, *shall* is used to express a simple statement – something you expect to happen:

I shall be in London next week.
We shall be pleased to see you.

If you put *will* after *I* or *we*, you express determination – you are going to make sure the thing does happen:

I will go; you can't stop me.
We will be heard; it is our right.

In the second and third persons, it is the other way round:

You will like it. (I hope)
You shall listen to me. (I'll make you listen.)

But nowadays this distinction is rarely made. Written *shall* seems to be on the way out, and in speech the distinction is blurred anyway:

I'll be in Scotland before you.

May and *might*

These two are confused and misused. *May* is the present-tense form and *might* is the past tense:

We think he may come. (it's still a possibility)
We thought he might come. (but he didn't)

In conditional sentences (sentences with *if*), *may* should be used only when the outcome is still unknown:

If he gets the last bus he may be back tonight.

But many people nowadays use *may* when they mean *might*, often with nonsensical results:

If the ambulance had not been so quick, I may have died.

Obviously the speaker didn't die, or he wouldn't be around to tell the tale. He meant:

If the ambulance had not been so quick, I might have died.

Gerund trouble

Grammarians have got it in for people who use the *-ing* form without bothering whether it's a participle or a gerund. Consider this sentence:

Mother doesn't like you speaking to me like that.

It isn't *you* that Mother doesn't like – it's your way of speaking. The rules require:

Mother doesn't like your speaking to me like that.

However, this construction may well be on the way out, even in writing.

Trouble with the infinitive

When grammarians started putting the English language into corsets, the perfect figure they had in mind for it was that of Latin grammar. In Latin an infinitive is a single word. But English infinitives are formed of two words, so in English you can split an infinitive apart with an adverb, as in *Star Trek*'s famous motto *to boldly go where no man has gone before.*

According to old-fashioned grammarians, that's a terrible way to treat a grammatical category. To make sure we keep to Latin ways, they invented the rule that you mustn't split an infinitive. It's a rule we break all the time in speaking, but when it comes to writing many people think they must obey it. They're wrong. An unsplit infinitive can be unclear:

The constable decided cautiously to approach the suspect.

Did he make this decision on grounds of prudence, or did he creep up quietly?

And compare these sentences:

He failed entirely to understand the question.
He failed to entirely understand the question.

These have quite different meanings, the second neatly conveyed by the split infinitive. No-one could argue that *He failed to understand entirely the question* is an improvement, while *He failed to understand the question entirely* is ambiguous – it doesn't tell us whether he understood partly, or not at all. So split your infinitives as much as you like.

Some tricky verbs

Many people confuse transitive and intransitive verbs that sound similar.

To wait is intransitive: you can't wait something; you just wait. *To await* is transitive and always needs an object:

They awaited the verdict with anxiety.

To lay is transitive and needs an object, except in the case of hens, who sometimes fail to lay (eggs, understood):

Today I lay my crown at your feet.
(present tense)

I laid myself open to criticism yesterday.
(past tense of *to lay*)

I have laid it out as clearly as possible.
(past participle of *to lay*)

To lie is intransitive and cannot have an object:

The apples lie rotting on the ground.
(present tense)

The soldiers lay where they had fallen.
(past tense of *to lie*)

They had lain there for weeks.
(past participle of *to lie*)

The past tense of *to lie* is *lay*, no matter who did the lying down. This is where the trouble starts. It sounds exactly like the present tense of *to lay* (apart from its third person singular, which, as in all verbs, ends in *-s*). This muddles people. They know that *lay* is involved somewhere in the verb *to lie*, and this leads them to use verb-forms suitable for laying a table to refer to lying down:

Why don't you go and lay down?
I laid on the bed.

The correct forms are:

Why don't you go and lie down?
I lay on the bed.

Confusing *lay* and *lie* is a mistake that peeves (and plenty of other people) are incredibly snooty about. They do have right on their side, although Lord Byron, no less, wrote: 'There let him lay.'

You shouldn't of…

If someone gives us an unexpected present, that's what we may say. At least, that's what it will *sound* as though we're saying. What we are really saying is *You shouldn't've*, which is the conversational form of *You should not have* [gone to so much trouble/spent so much/felt you needed to, etc.].

People who do not understand the structure of past-tense verbs only reveal this when they write. They put down what they hear, or rather what they think they hear:

> She could of got here earlier.
> He may of missed the way.

This is an elementary grammatical mistake which will not make a good impression at all.

Adjectives are words that describe nouns or pronouns. They can come before the noun they describe, or after it:

We had a delicious meal.
Wash those dirty hands!

Petals, red, pink and white, fluttered to the ground.

They can act as the complement of the verb *to be*:

Not all people are honest.

They can stand alone and act like a noun:

The Dutch are going to the polls.
The number of unemployed has risen.
You take the green one; I'll have the yellow.

The present or past participle of a verb can be used as an adjective:

61

I was glad to see a smiling face.
He had a decided advantage over the others.

Adjectives can be reinforced by adverbs, to define or intensify their meaning:

clearly incorrect, surprisingly popular, extremely poor

As well as their normal form, adjectives have two other forms that are used to compare one noun with another. *Rich*, for instance, has a comparative form, *richer*, and a superlative form, *richest*.

Most adjectives of one syllable, and those of two syllables that end in *-y* or *-er*, follow this pattern:

Ann is luckier than her brother.
She is the cleverest of all.

Adjectives of several syllables make their comparatives with *more* and their superlatives with *most*:

Chess is more difficult than draughts.
This chair is the most comfortable.

Some adjectives alter form completely in the comparative and superlative:

good, better, best
bad, worse, worst
little, less, least
much, more, most
far, further, furthest (or farther, farthest)

Trouble with adjectives

• Hold them tight. Keep them close to the noun they describe, to avoid ambiguities like this:

Chest-hugging ladies' jumpers.

• Don't let them gush. Some adjectives have alternative comparative and superlative forms:

lovelier/more lovely; cleverer/more clever

Choose one or the other, never both: *He is the most cleverest* will not do.

• False comparisons. When speaking of amounts and quantities, we never muddle *little* and *few*:

She has few ideas.
She has little imagination.

Few applies to things that can be counted; *little* applies to things that cannot.

63

Yet, when it comes to comparisons, the distinction is often forgotten. *Fewer* is increasingly given the boot and *less* grabs its job. Don't let it. The familiar supermarket sign *Baskets with less than 5 items* should read *fewer than 5 items*. At least one High Street retailer has corrected its signs, to the delight of language sticklers.

Pet peeve

• *He is taller than me* or *He is taller than I*? Traditional grammarians agree that only *taller than I* is correct here, though to most of us nowadays this sounds rather stilted. You can always avoid the problem by writing *He is taller than I am*; no-one can object to this.

• Be absolutely right. The meaning of certain adjectives (termed 'absolutes') prevents them from having a comparative or superlative. You can eat a whole apple but you cannot eat one that is *wholer* or *wholest*. *Complete*, *square*, *perfect*, *final* and *unique* are other examples.

Pet peeve

Misuse of *unique* can make the peevologists foam. A thing is 'unique' if there is no other example of it in existence, so 'more unique' and 'very unique' are meaningless expressions.

Just as an adjective describes a noun, so an adverb describes the action denoted by a verb. Most adverbs are formed by adding *-ly* to an adjective:

slowly, sincerely, unfortunately, definitely

But there are plenty of exceptions. Some of these exceptions give information about time, place or manner:

I told her to do it *then*.
They will be ready *tomorrow*.

Come *outside*.
We did not see him *there*.

Stand *fast*.
Hold on *tight*.

Some apply to whole sentences:

Anyway, it won't cost much.

65

An adverb can come between a verb and its auxiliary:

We have often debated this matter.

But it shouldn't come between the verb and its object, as in *We have debated often this matter*.

It can come before the verb or after its object:

We completely demolished their argument.
We demolished their argument completely.

But keep it before the object if the object has a long clause attached, as here:

We completely demolished their argument that there was no profit to be made from the business this year.

Except in a few colloquial expressions, such as *dead easy*, that you wouldn't use in formal writing, an adjective is not a suitable replacement for an adverb:

The home team pressed more strongly [not *stronger*] towards the end of play.

Trouble with adverbs

Avoid placing an adverb where it will be ambiguous:

He disliked extremely off-hand manners.

Did all bad manners make him absolutely furious, or was it only the worst sort?

Pet peeve

The adverb *only* likes to cling to the verb, but peevologists insist it must go where the sense needs it. They claim that *He only spoke for ten minutes* means that he did nothing else during that time. Actually, there is rarely a problem, but sometimes its position really does matter:

I only lent you the book yesterday.
(I didn't make you a present of it.)

I lent only you the book yesterday.
(No-one else got a copy.)

I lent you the only book yesterday.
(It was my sole copy.)

I lent you the book only yesterday.
(I don't expect you to return it yet.)

The best rule with *only* is that, provided it makes your meaning clear, you should put it wherever it sounds most natural.

Drifting adverbs

Hopefully is a drifter that gets peevologists hopping mad. It has a way of hanging about at the beginning of a sentence in which it has no connection at all with the verb:

Hopefully she will be back in time for supper.

This doesn't mean that she is returning in a hopeful frame of mind, but simply that the speaker hopes she will be back.

Oddly enough, people who find *hopefully* offensive usually don't object to similar adverbial phrases such as *surprisingly*, *admittedly* or *thankfully*. This is probably because these expressions have been around for such a long time that no-one queries their grammatical credentials.

The safest policy is never to use *hopefully* in this way in writing. Best practice would be not to say it either. Say *I'm hoping she'll be back in time* instead.

English loves to make new verbs by tacking prepositions onto old ones. Pity the poor learner of English who has to grapple with their meanings! For instance, see what prepositions can do for the simple verb *to look*. We can:

look for (search for, or expect)
look up (in a dictionary)
look up to (a person)
look forward to (an event)
look over (a premises)
look after (an invalid)
look down on (inferiors)
look into (investigate)
look in on (visit someone informally)
look by (make a visit in passing)
look on (be a spectator)
look out (be careful)
look through (sort or study, as of papers)

We do that sort of thing with lots of verbs. See how many you can make from *put*, or *stand*.

A spot of trouble with prepositions

Prepositions do a simple job, so they don't give much trouble. Even so, when grammarians drew up the rules they couldn't let prepositions alone.

• Because Latin sentences cannot end with a preposition, grammarians came up with the rule that you must not end an English sentence with one either. Conscientiously following the rule can produce uncomfortable sentences such as:

The police report revealed nothing about from which window he fell.
('. . . which window he fell from' sounds much more natural.)

The best thing to do with this rule is to ignore it. Sir Winston Churchhill said all there is to say on the matter when he allegedly marked an official's report with 'This is the sort of English up with which I will not put.'

Feel comfortable with prepositions and put them where you like – though it may be best not to imitate the nurse who asked her charge:

What did you choose that book to be read to out of for?

• The preposition *of* is entirely redundant in sentences like these; cut it out:

> Their house is outside of the catchment area.
> I could get it done inside of a week.
> Can you get the top off of this bottle?

• *Different from* or *different to*?

> That is a different version from the one I heard.
> That is a different method to the one I use.

Different from is currently regarded as the correct form, though both are used in speech.

There is a third version going around these days: *different than*. Although in American English it is acceptable to say *My aims now are different than they were at the start of the project*, in British English it is emphatically not (you have to say *different from what they were*). But perhaps it will be one day.

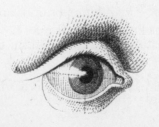

Conjunctions

These come in two flavours according to the work they do:

• Co-ordinating conjunctions, like *and*, *but* and *or*, link parts of a sentence that are doing similar grammatical jobs:

He is tall and fair. (two adjectives)

There's a footprint but no sign of the culprit. (a noun and a noun phrase)

She said she'd be there very shortly, or as soon as possible. (two adverbial phrases)

He knew he was wrong and he wouldn't admit it. (two main clauses)

• Subordinating conjunctions link a subordinate clause with a main clause. *When*, *where*, *so that* and *although* are examples of subordinating conjunctions. They introduce clauses that provide additional information about the main verb, such as how, when, where or why its action is taking place. You can see the various kinds of subordinating conjunctions in action in the next section, on clauses.

Trouble with conjunctions

• Conjunctions usually give little trouble. However, *and* sometimes muscles in where it has no business:

> I'll try and get it done in a week.
> Wait and see what he says.

In speech this is perfectly acceptable, but in writing it's best to use the more traditional form with the infinitive:

> I'll try to get it done.
> Wait to see what he says.

• There used to be an idea that, in writing, it was clumsy to start a sentence with *and* or *but*. Now it is perfectly all right to do so. Opening with *and* is a good way of indicating that what is coming next will reinforce what has just been said. But don't do it too often, of course.

Subordinate clauses provide more information about the subject, the verb or the object in the main clause.

Adverbial clauses add information about the verb. They behave like adverbs, but can say more than an adverb on its own.

• Adverbial clauses of time tell you when the action of the verb happened. They are introduced by the subordinating conjunctions *before, after, until, when*:

I made a cup of tea before I went to bed.

• Adverbial clauses of place, saying where it happened, are introduced by *where* or *wherever*:

I left my teacup where I usually do.

• Adverbial clauses of reason, explaining why it happened, are introduced by *because, since* or *as*:

As I was thirsty, I made a cup of tea.

74

• Adverbial clauses of manner, telling how it happened, are introduced by *as if* or *as though*:

They drank their tea as if they were parched.

• Adverbial clauses of purpose show the purpose of the action described in the main clause:

I rinsed the cups so that they could go in the dishwasher.

• Adverbial clauses of result show what results from the action of the main clause:

The tea was so hot that I burned my tongue.

• Adverbial clauses of condition state the conditions under which something will be done:

I'll make some tea if you will clear up.

• Adverbial clauses of comparison are introduced by *as . . . as* or *than*:

I drink as much tea as he does.
I drink a lot more tea than she does.

• Adverbial clauses of concession are introduced by *though*, *although*, *even if*:

I drank the tea although it was nearly cold.

75

Adjectival clauses do the same work as adjectives. They tell you more about a noun in the main clause and are introduced by a relative pronoun, so called because it 'relates' the clause to the word it is describing. Examples of relative pronouns are *which, that, who, whose, whom. Which* and *that* relate to things, while the others are used of people.

Adjectival clauses can relate to the subject of the sentence:

The one who runs fastest will get fruit gums.

They can relate to the object of the verb:

I beat Stephen, whom everyone had expected to win. (Note that *who* changes to *whom* when it relates to the object.)

I won a bag that had no blackcurrant gums.

Someone has taken my fruit gums, which I had put away in my pocket.

Or they can relate to a noun in a subordinate clause:

I was planning to share those gums with my brother, who will be home tomorrow.

The relative pronoun *that* can often be left out without causing any confusion:

Those were the fruit gums [that] I won at the church bazaar.

Trouble with clauses

• *Which* and *that*: are they interchangeable? Often they are, but there is a traditional rule on the matter and you are quite likely to be obeying it instinctively. It says *that* is used in 'defining clauses' and *which* in 'commenting clauses'.

If you say *The coat that came from Italy was widely admired*, you are using a defining clause: it defines which coat you mean. You may have others that were not admired.

If you say *The coat, which was double-breasted, with brass buttons, was widely admired*, you are using a commenting clause that simply pops in extra information about the noun it relates to.

Keeping to this rule in formal writing will win you Brownie points. As in the examples above, a commenting clause should be within commas; a defining one should not.

• *Since* and *because* are used by most people as if they were interchangeable. Whenever there is a risk of ambiguity, *because* should be used for clauses of reason and *since* should be reserved for clauses of time:

Because I was unhappy, I couldn't stay in a job.

Since I have been in Italy, I have had numerous jobs.

• *If* and *whether* should not be confused. *Whether* expresses a condition which can be fufilled in two different ways. *If* expresses a condition where there is no alternative:

She'll come whether it rains or not.
(Two possibilities are mentioned.)

She won't come if it rains.
(Only one possibility is mentioned.)

In some cases *if* cannot be used without the risk of misunderstanding. If you get an invitation ending *Please let me know if you can come*, you could (if you are feeling bloody-minded) take this to mean that if you can't come, you don't need to reply. The invitation should have read:

Please let me know whether you can come.

Who and *whom*

There is no doubt that *whom* is on the way out in everyday speech. People think it's stuffy. Someone said it was invented to make you sound like a butler. But peevologists are keeping up a fierce rearguard action. They point out that *who* should only be used when it is the subject of the verb in its clause:

> The singer who performed last night was outstanding.

When it is the object of the verb, its objective form, *whom*, should used:

> The singer whom I heard last night was outstanding.

Careful speakers still observe this rule. But they tend to draw the line at sentences requiring *to whom*. They are not likely to say *I can't remember to whom I gave it*. The preferred form is *I can't remember who I gave it to*.

In writing a formal letter or report, you will not brand yourself as a ridiculous old peeve if you use *whom* wherever it is correct. In a formal context it is the right thing to do.

Like

Like is a preposition. In formal English it is not allowed to assume the airs of a subordinating conjunction and introduce a clause. You can say:

> I can't work in the evening like Sidney.
> She ran like the devil.

Here the preposition like is merely attaching a noun to the sentence.

But you should not say:

> I can't work in the evening like Sidney does.
> She ran like she had the devil on her tail.

In these examples, *like* is followed by a verb, which means that the words coming after it form a clause. They are adverbial clauses of manner, which should be introduced by the subordinating conjunctions *as*, *as if* or *as though*:

> I can't work in the evening as Sidney does.
> She ran as if she had the devil on her tail.

(In American English it is acceptable to use *like* to introduce a clause. This use is creeping into British English too, but it has not become respectable yet.)

80

Negatives

In some languages, negatives (*not*, *never*, etc.) back each other up: two of them make an even stronger denial. But traditional English grammar takes the view that two negatives cancel one another out, so *I didn't say nothing* means 'I did say something.' And sentences like these can take some unravelling:

I shouldn't be surprised if it doesn't rain.

Its importance cannot be underestimated.

Let it not be supposed, because we are building for the future rather than the present, that the Bill's proposals are not devoid of significance.

That last one comes from a speech in the House of Lords. What the speaker meant was:

Let it not be supposed that they *are* devoid of significance. (that is, they are significant)

81

Take care with the placing of *not*. It can cause confusion in sentences containing *every* or *because*:

Every member of the choir was not present.

Does this mean that they were all absent or that not all of them were there? Better to say *Not every member of the choir was present.*

I did not go because of what Sarah said.

Did what Sarah said put you off, or are you saying that your going had nothing to do with her influence? If the former, better to say *Because of what Sarah said, I did not go.*

Peevologists insist that *neither . . . nor* should not be used when there are more than two options; they allow *neither here nor there*, but not *neither here nor there nor anywhere*. Take no notice of them.

Carry your negatives through – don't lose sight of them after *and*. Here's a genuine example from a news website, about flights being delayed by bad weather:

'It is vital that passengers do not make their way to the airport and check our website and with their airline for updates,' she added.

Obviously it's vital that they *do* check; the spokesperson should have said:

It is vital that passengers do not make their way to the airport and *that they* check our website and *check* with their airline for updates.

(The double use of *check* in the original quotation is an instance of the figure of speech known as *zeugma* or *syllepsis*, which is outside the scope of this book. The classic example is 'She left in a huff and a taxi.')

A reminder

If you remember that none *means* not one, *you won't be tempted to give it a plural verb.*

American English

Grammatical differences between British and American English are few.

Where an American will say *Do you have a pen?* a speaker of British English will ask *Have you a pen?* or *Have you got a pen?* This use of *I have got* meaning 'I possess' is not usual in the States. There, the verb *to get* is used more often in the sense of 'to obtain', in which case its past participle is *gotten* (no longer used in British English, though it was in Shakespeare's day):

They've gotten a good price for it.

Americans are more tolerant of adjectives used adverbially:

Sure!
That's real nice of you.

Differences in vocabulary are not likely to lead to major misunderstandings, but…

• Most British English speakers know that a *bum* in American is a tramp, that *gas* is petrol, a *pacifier* is a dummy and *suspenders* are braces, though they may not know that *knickers* are a type of trousers.

• Differences may sometimes raise a smile. *Backside* in British English means what Americans call your *ass*, while in American it refers to the rear of a building. The people of Sod City, West Virginia, see nothing odd in its name, which derives from the local word for a bog; while *bog*, in the UK, can refer to a lavatory.

• Very rarely there is a stumbling block. In British usage the verb *to slate* means to criticise severely. In American it means to 'pencil in' provisionally, as on a slate, so *The manager has been slated for today's meeting* is open to serious misinterpretation.

Discriminatory language

This is a danger area, because ignorance will not be accepted as an excuse.

Mongol is no longer an acceptable term for a person with Down's syndrome. Speakers of British English are aware by now that *Red Indian* is not the way to refer to a Native American. But they may not know that *spook*, which to them means a ghost (or a spy), is an offensive term to apply to someone black in America.

Sensitivity to these issues sometimes causes problems with perfectly innocent words. *Niggardly*, for example, has nothing whatever to do with race or colour. It comes from an Old Norse word meaning 'stingy'. Such words shouldn't offend, but, when communicating with people who might misunderstand them, they are probably best avoided.

With sexist language it's a question of being sensitive to people's feelings and not putting their backs up. When inviting someone you don't know well, you're nowadays quite likely to add 'Do bring your partner,' since *partner* is understood to mean one half of a close relationship, no matter which sexes are involved. Nowadays, when you mean 'business partner', you have to say so explicitly.

We saw on pages 32–33 how it's possible to be non-sexist with uncooperative English pronouns, by using the grammatically incorrect *their* when the gender of the possessor is unclear. Similarly, it's best to address a woman as *Ms* in writing if you don't know whether she is married or might resent the matter being noted. You can't use it in speech, though – it's unpronounceable.

Train yourself to use gender-neutral words wherever appropriate: *actor* in place of *actress*, *flight attendant* for *air hostess*, *bartender* for *barman*, *the human race* for *mankind*, and so forth. But, again, don't be oversensitive. *Mandate, management* and *manipulate* have no connection with *man* – nor has *manure*!

Let this be a warning

Overzealous use of non-sexist language can occasionally backfire. In the Guardian's *obituary for the Italian film director Carlo Ponti, the paper's style guide caused it to say that in his early career Ponti was 'already a man with a good eye for pretty actors'. It might, for once, have been better to say 'actresses'.*

Danglers and floaters

Floaters, danglers and garden-path sentences are the grammatical equivalent of opening your mouth and putting your foot in it. They are perpetrated by people who don't think their sentences through.

Floating phrases

When you use a descriptive phrase, attach it closely to the noun or pronoun it relates to; otherwise it will be left floating. It will hitch itself to the nearest thing and make nonsense of your sentence:

When over 75, the government does not require you to have a TV licence. (Will the present government be that long in office?)

Since he was begging so appealingly, he gave the dog a slice. (Perhaps the dog had trained him to beg?)

Absolute phrases vs. dangling participles

The present participle ending in *-ing* has to refer to a noun or pronoun within the sentence:

> Having cleared the streets, the police restored order.

This sentence is in order, because both the clearing and the restoring were done by the same subject, the police.

An 'absolute' phrase stands outside the structure of the main sentence, as if in invisible grammatical brackets:

> The police having cleared the streets, order was restored.

This sentence is also correct. The rule with absolute phrases is that their present participle must have an identifiable subject within the phrase. In this case it is *the police*.

Grammatical mayhem starts when a writer embarks on an absolute phrase and then forgets to give it a subject. The present participle clings to whatever is available:

Driving through Lincolnshire, clumps of large-flowered modern daffodils planted by district councils mar the verges.

Watch out for those motor-powered vandalising daffodils! Militant anti-peevers say this sort of thing only matters if it's misleading. Everyone knows that daffodils can't drive, so why the fuss? Grammar purists point out that it's a sign of sloppy thinking.

Garden-path sentences

These don't actually break any rules, but mislead the reader into thinking a sentence is heading one way when it's really going somewhere else:

The government plans to raise taxes were defeated.

The greyhound raced down the track collapsed.

False associations

Certain words are so often found linked together that when we spot them coming up in a sentence our mind automatically joins them up. It's disconcerting to discover midway that, in this particular case, they're having nothing to do with each other:

Behind each part of the story *I shall tell lies* an unsuspected tale of hard work.

A tale of the devious and *the dirty behind* which such people take refuge.

Headline howlers

Headline writers have to take short cuts. Even so, they should be on grammar alert:

POLICE CHIEF'S PLEDGE TO MURDER WITNESS

The writer has used the noun *murder* as an adjective, forgetting that it can be a verb as well.

SON BLAMED FOR THEFT BY FATHER

Did the father accuse, or did he steal?

BRITON MAULED BY TIGER IN INTENSIVE CARE

How did the tiger get in there?

GENERAL FLIES BACK TO FRONT

In this classic headline, the unintended meaning comes across so strongly that it is genuinely difficult to work out what was really meant – that the general is returning to the war zone by aeroplane.

COMPLAINTS ABOUT REFEREES GROWING UGLY

This can't be improved on – it's perfect of its kind.

And finally...

Make of this what you will:

The witness stated that she had seen sexual intercourse taking place between the parked vans.

adjective A 'describing word' used to give information about a noun or pronoun.

adverb A 'describing word' used with a verb to say how something is done. Most English adverbs end in *-ly*.

agreement The rule by which a verb must match its subject in person and number, and a pronoun must match its antecedent in number and gender.

auxiliary verb A verb such as *have, be, may, will, shall*, which helps other verbs to form various tenses.

case A distinctive form of a noun or pronoun indicating its relationship to other words in a sentence.

clause A sequence of words, consisting of a subject and a predicate, that is part of a larger sentence.

complement The part of a predicate that follows the verb *to be* (except when it is used as an auxiliary).

conjunction A linking word such as *and, or, but, yet, while*.

gerund A verbal noun ending in *-ing*.

infinitive The basic form of a verb, often preceded by *to*, which does not indicate number or tense.

inflection A distinctive ending given to a word to indicate its relationship to other words in the sentence.

interjection A word or phrase used to express a state of mind, but having no grammatical function.

noun A 'naming word' that refers to a person, thing, place or concept.

object A noun or pronoun that names the person or thing to which the action denoted by the verb is done.

participle A verb form that functions as an adjective, while also indicating present or past tense. Present participles end in -*ing*; regular past participles end in -*ed*.

phrase A group of words which are connected together but do not amount to a clause.

predicate The part of a clause that is not the subject; it always contains a finite verb, and the object of the verb if it has one.

preposition A word such as *at, in, by, down, under*, which expresses the relationship of a noun or pronoun to some other person, thing or action in the sentence.

pronoun A word that stands in for a noun, to avoid repetition.

sentence A sequence of words, consisting of at least a subject and a predicate, that is sufficient by itself to form a statement or question.

subject A noun or pronoun that names the person or thing carrying out the action denoted by the verb.

subordinate clause A clause that provides additional information but cannot stand by itself as a main clause. It is typically introduced by a conjunction such as *if, when, which, although*.

tense The form of a verb that indicates the point in time (past, present, future) at which its action is taking place.

verb A 'doing word' that names an action. A verb may be **finite**, having a subject and a tense, and able to form part of a main clause; **active**, having an object affected by its action; **passive**, expressing an action experienced by the subject; **subjunctive**, expressing a supposition or a hypothetical action; **imperative**, expressing a command or exhortation; **transitive**, expressing an action affecting a subject or object; **intransitive**, expressing an action that is complete in itself and does not affect an object.